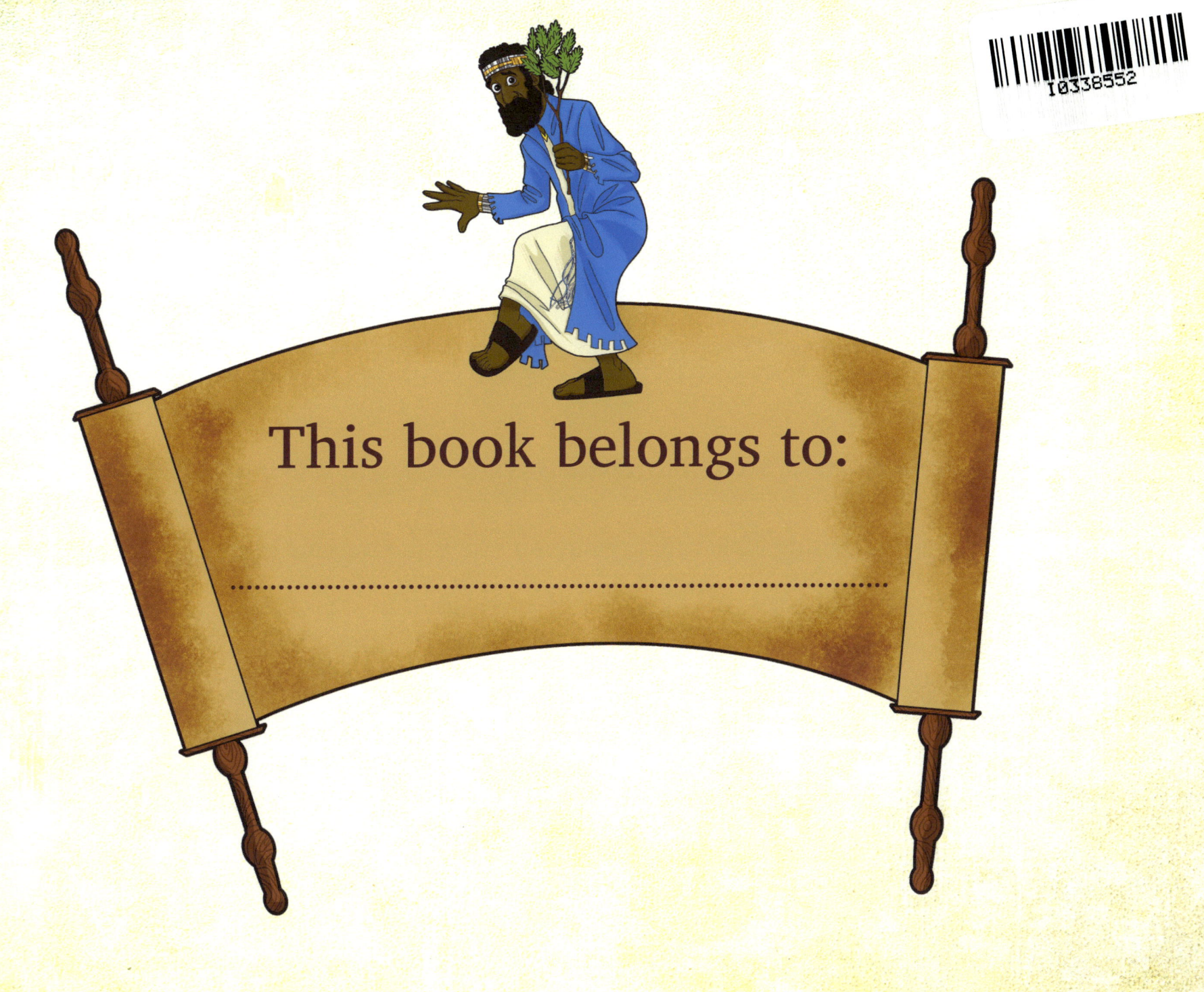

This book belongs to:

....

Copyright © BPA Publishing Ltd 2020

Author: Pip Reid
Illustrator: Thomas Barnett
Creative Director: Curtis Reid

www.biblepathwayadventures.com

Thank you for supporting Bible Pathway Adventures®. Our adventure series helps parents teach their children more about the Bible in a fun creative way. Designed for the whole family, Bible Pathway Adventures' mission is to help bring discipleship back into homes around the world. The search for truth is more fun than tradition!

The moral rights of author and illustrator have been asserted, this book is copyright.

ISBN: 978-0-473-38453-1

Witch of Endor

The adventures of King Saul

"There shall not be found among you anyone who burns his son or daughter as an offering, anyone who practices divination or tells fortunes or interprets omens, or a sorcerer or a charmer or a medium or a necromancer or one who inquires of the dead..." (Deuteronomy 18:10-11)

Long ago when judges ruled the land of Israel, there lived a great Hebrew judge named Samuel. Samuel was much more than a judge; he was a prophet and an army commander, too!

When Samuel grew older, he made judges of his sons to help him rule the people. But his sons did whatever they pleased. They loved money more than God and made bad decisions if money was secretly given to them as a bribe. The Israelites grew tired of the sons' bad behavior. They came to Samuel and said, "You are old and your sons behave badly. Give us a king to rule over us like other nations."

"You do not need a king to rule you," said Samuel angrily. "Yah, the god of Abraham, Isaac, and Jacob, is your king." But no matter what he said, the people would not listen and insisted on a king.

To Samuel's surprise, God said to him, "Listen to the people and do everything they say. Give them a king, but warn them what a king will do."

"A king will make your lives miserable," Samuel told the people. "He will take a tenth of your grain and flocks, and you will become his slaves." However, the Israelites covered their ears and would not listen. "Give us a king to rule over us," they said.

Samuel did not dare choose a king himself. He waited for God to pick the right man for the job. Out of the twelve tribes of Israel, God chose a man named Saul. He was tall and handsome, and looked just like a king. "God has made you king of the Israelites," Samuel told Saul. He poured a flask of olive oil over Saul's head to anoint him as king. "Your job is to rule the people and protect them from all their enemies."

Did you know?

Many people believe there are different ways to pronounce God's name. These include Yah, Yahweh, Yahuah, and many others.

Samuel gathered the people of Israel at Mizpeh to greet their new king. "Because you rejected God as your king, God has chosen a man named Saul from the tribe of Benjamin to rule you," he said.

You might think Saul would be filled with excitement about becoming a king. Instead he was very afraid. He hid among the tents so he could not be found. The Israelites ran and brought him before the people. "This is the man God has chosen," shouted Samuel. "Long live the king of Israel!" everyone shouted back.

Saul didn't know what it meant to be a king. Whenever he wanted to know what to do next, he asked God for answers. Sometimes God answered him in a dream, sometimes He used His High Priest, and sometimes He used His prophet Samuel. But Saul didn't always listen to God.

Did you know?

King Saul was the tallest man in the land of Israel. He was nearly seven meters tall! (1 Samuel 9:2)

One day, Saul gathered the Israelites together at Gilgal to fight their enemies, the fearsome Philistines. The Philistines had thousands of chariots, and more soldiers than you could count. Saul's soldiers were terrified. They ran for their lives and hid in caves and watchtowers and holes in the ground.

Samuel sent a message to Saul. "Do not go into battle until we have made a sacrifice to God." But after many days Samuel still had not come to perform the sacrifice. Saul did not wait any longer. He made the sacrifice himself. Just as he finished, Samuel arrived. "What have you done?" he cried.

"The Philistines are ready to attack and my soldiers are running away," said Saul. "You did not come when you said you would, so I made the sacrifice."

"You fool!" said Samuel. "If you had obeyed God's instructions, He would have let you and your descendants rule Israel forever. Because you disobeyed Him, God will find another man to rule the kingdom of Israel."

Many years passed, and Samuel grew old and weak. When he died, all the Israelites gathered to bury him in his hometown of Ramah. Saul was sad, too. "Who will help me rule the people of Israel?" he said. He feared it wouldn't be long before the Philistines attacked the Israelites again.

Saul did not have to wait long. Once again the Philistines appeared in the distance, ready for battle. When Saul saw the huge Philistine army, his heart trembled with fear. There were even more soldiers and chariots than before.

"What am I going to do?" cried Saul. He needed God's help fast! He tried to talk to God, but God did not answer him – not by dreams, nor prophets, nor the High Priest. All he heard was silence.

Did you know?

Samuel was a Nazarite. He was dedicated to God as a child and never cut his hair. (1 Samuel 1:11)

King Saul tossed and turned in his bed all night. *Why does God not answer me?* he wondered. *If Samuel were here, he would tell me what to do.*

Before long, Saul came up with a terrible plan. Even though he had forced witches and wizards to leave the land of Israel, he said to his servants, "Find a woman who tells the future by talking to dead people. Perhaps she can tell me how to defeat our enemies."

"There is a witch who lives in a cave near Endor," said a servant. "Let's go and see her." Saul's eyes lit up. He liked the idea. "Yes! She can talk to Samuel for me," he said. But God was not pleased with Saul's plan.

Saul wasted no time. He tore off his battle armor and put on a special disguise so no one would know that he was the king.

That night after dark, Saul and his servants crept out of the camp and headed for Endor. They tiptoed past soldiers ready for battle, and along narrow stony roads full of holes. A black cloud crept over the moon, and a cold wind began to blow. It was a dark and dangerous journey.

Soon an enormous cave appeared before them. "This is where the witch of Endor lives," said one of Saul's servants. The men stopped outside the entrance and peered inside. "Is anyone there?" Saul shouted into the cave. "You have nothing to fear. Come outside."

All of a sudden, a figure dressed in black stepped out of the cave. Her long grey hair blew loose in the wind. Saul and the men gasped. They could hardly believe their eyes. Standing in front of them was the wicked witch of Endor.

The witch looked the men up and down. Pointing a finger angrily at Saul, she said, "Who are you? What do you want from me?" Saul had never felt so nervous in his entire life. He took a deep breath. "Tell me the future," he said. "Bring up the person I tell you from the dead."

The witch peered at Saul suspiciously. "The king has forced witches to leave the land of Israel. Are you trying to trick me and get me killed?" She did not recognize Saul in his old woolen cloak. His clever disguise had worked!

Did you know?

God forbids witchcraft. God clearly commanded His people never to consult a witch or medium, but Saul ignored this instruction. (Leviticus 19:31)

"Do not worry," Saul said to the witch. He wrapped his cloak tightly around him. "As God lives, you will not get in trouble with the king for doing this." The witch scratched her chin and thought for a moment. "Whom shall I bring up for you?" she asked. "Bring up the prophet Samuel," answered Saul.

Grabbing Saul by the arm, the witch led the men into the cave. They looked around in amazement. Giant cobwebs stretched out across the walls. A fire crackled in the center. Jars filled with potions glowed in the light.

Saul paced back and forth across the cave. "We cannot waste another minute," he said. "Bring up the prophet Samuel now."

Flashing Saul a wicked smile, the witch bent over the crackling fire and began chanting strange words. Saul's heart thudded with fear. He knew it was wrong to try to talk to the dead.

Before long, ghostly figures began to appear outside the cave. When the witch saw Samuel, she screamed and said to Saul, "Why have you tricked me? You must be the king of Israel!"

"Don't be afraid," said Saul. "Tell me what you see." The witch stared at the glowing figures in horror. "I see god-like beings coming up from the earth." Saul's eyes grew wide. "What do they look like?" he asked. "There is an old man wearing a robe," said the witch.

Saul looked out through the mist at the old man. "This must be the prophet, Samuel," he said. He fell to the ground, full of fear.

"Saul, what are you doing?" thundered Samuel. "Why did you wake me from my sleep?" Saul scrambled to his feet and stared anxiously at Samuel. "I am in big trouble," he said. "The Philistines are ready to attack us. God doesn't talk to me anymore. Not by prophets or dreams. What shall I do?"

"Why are you asking me?" said Samuel. "There is nothing you can do. You disobeyed God and He gave your kingdom to another man. God has declared that you and your sons will soon die, and the Philistines will defeat your army."

Without another word, Samuel disappeared back into the earth. Saul was so afraid that he could not speak. His legs turned to jelly and he fell down to the ground again. He did not want to fight the fearsome Philistines at all!

Did you know?

Samuel was the last judge of Israel. (Acts 13:20) He anointed the first two kings of Israel: Saul and David.

Before Saul and the men returned to the battlefield, the witch cooked them a meal to give Saul strength. Then they hurried back to the camp to face the mighty Philistines.

Early the next morning, the Philistines attacked the Israelites again. In a thundering roar and great cloud of dust, they charged onto the battlefield with their chariots and horses.

The Israelites were filled with panic. They ran away as fast as they could. But the Philistines were determined to kill Saul. They chased after him with swords and arrows, and sharp weapons made of bronze.

Did you know?

The Philistines were very religious. They celebrated victories in their temples, and often carried their idol gods into battle. These false gods included Dagon, the fish god. (2 Samuel 5:21)

As Saul and his armor bearer scrambled up a steep cliff, a Philistine soldier shot him with his arrows. The king crashed to the ground with a mighty thud.

THOOMP!

Saul lay on his back and stared up at the sky. He knew the Israelites were no match for the mighty Philistines. Turning to his armor bearer, he said, "Kill me with your sword. If the Philistines capture me, they will torture me until I'm dead." The armor bearer shook his head. "No," he said. "I dare not kill the king of Israel."

Saul could not wait any longer. Taking his own sword, he threw himself upon it. When his armor bearer saw that Saul was dead, he did the same thing and died with him. And so it happened that Saul and his three sons died that day, just as Samuel had said.

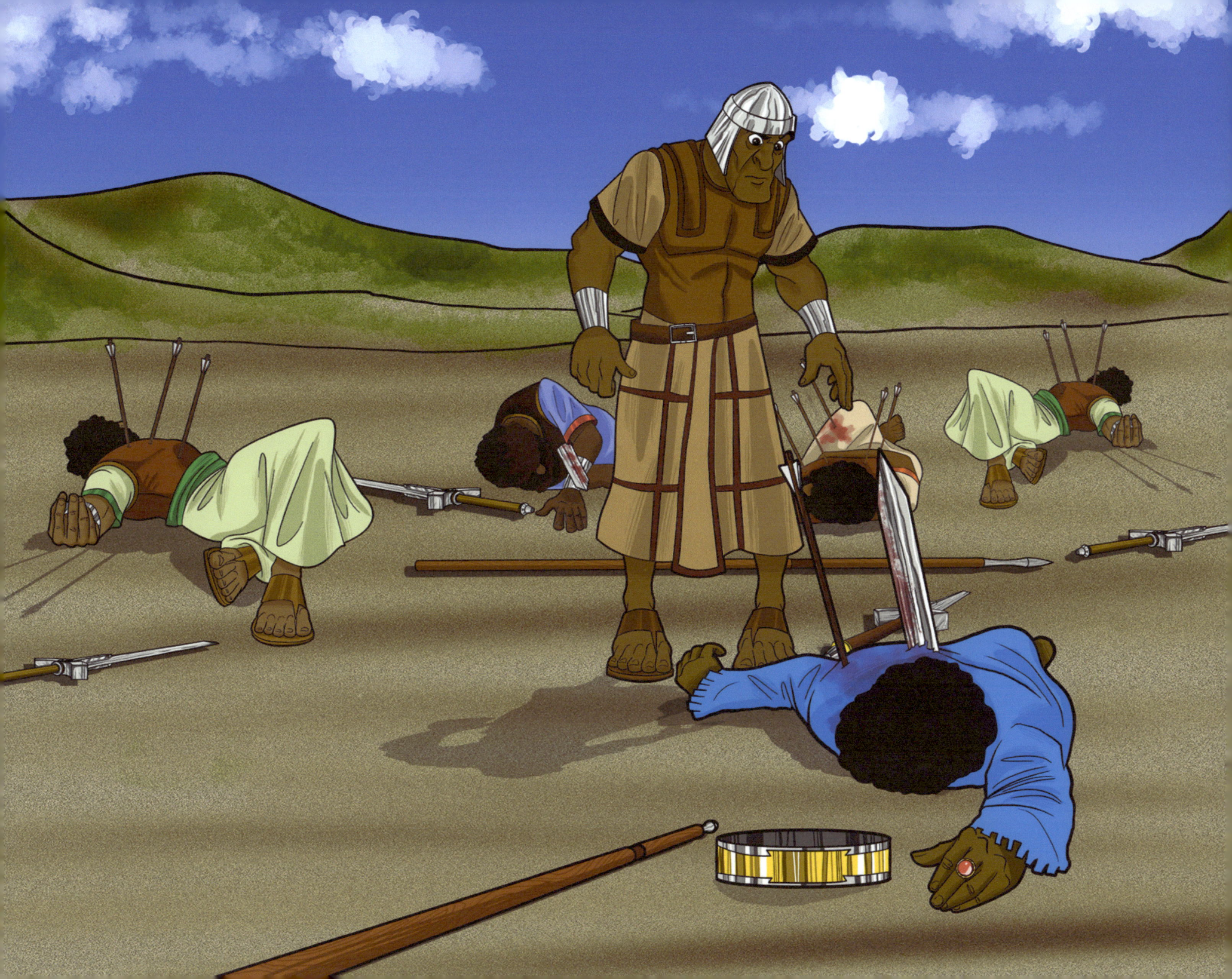

The next day, the Philistines returned to the battlefield. They found the bodies of Saul and his sons lying on the ground. The soldiers chopped off their heads and hung their bodies on the city wall at Beth-shan for everyone to see.

News of Saul's death spread quickly throughout the land of Israel. When the people of the town of Jabesh Gilead heard about their dead king, they were angry.

"How dare the Philistines kill our brave king!" they shouted. "We must find him and bring him home!"

Did you know?

During this time, there were no blacksmiths in the land of Israel. The Israelites took their iron tools to the Philistines to get sharpened.
(1 Samuel 13:20)

The strongest men from the village sprang into action. That night while everyone was sleeping, they leapt on horses and hurried to Beth-shan. Taking the bodies of Saul and his sons down from the city wall, they tied them onto their horses and raced back home before the Philistines even knew the bodies were gone.

That week the Israelites buried Saul and his sons under a tree in the village. They wept and mourned for their beloved king. They could hardly believe the king of Israel was dead.

Even kings need to trust and obey God's instructions, and follow His Ways.

THE END

TEST YOUR KNOWLEDGE!

(Match the question with the answer at the bottom of the page)

QUESTIONS

King Saul was king of which people? ....

Which army wanted to fight the Israelites? ....

Why did King Saul want to talk to a witch? ....

In which town did King Saul talk to a witch? ....

Who did King Saul ask the witch to raise from the grave? ....

Why did King Saul want to talk to Samuel? ....

What did Samuel tell King Saul? ....

Where in the Bible does Yah forbid trying to talk to dead people? ....

What happened to King Saul after he visited the witch of Endor? ....

How did King Saul lose his life? ....

ANSWERS

1. The Philistines
2. Endor
3. Deuteronomy 18
4. Saul and his sons will lose their lives
5. Fell on his sword
6. The Israelites
7. Went into battle against the Philistines
8. The prophet Samuel
9. To understand the future
10. To learn how to defeat the Philistines

Complete the Word Search Puzzle

SAUL   PHILISTINES
ENDOR ISRAELITES
WITCH KING
PROPHET BATTLE
SAMUEL ARMY

```
E F F B F P K P W I
P N K S C D D H P S
R Q D X A D O I B R
O X B O J U Z L K A
P R J K R C L I I E
H A A R M Y P S N L
E W I T C H K T G I
T P I A L X H I T T
S A M U E L X N E E
B A T T L E D E D S
```

Bible Pathway Adventures®

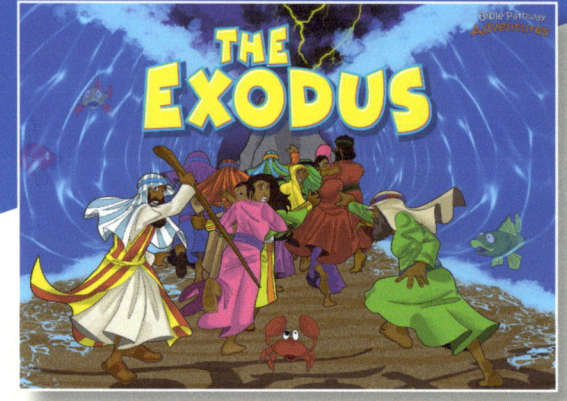

The Exodus
Escape from Egypt
The Great Flood
Thrown to the Lions
The Chosen Bride
Swallowed by a Fish
Saved by a Donkey
Samson Mighty Warrior
Facing the Giant
Birth of the King
Betrayal of the King
The Risen King
Shipwrecked!

Discover more Bible Pathway Adventures' Bible stories!

Check out Bible Pathway Adventures' Activity Books

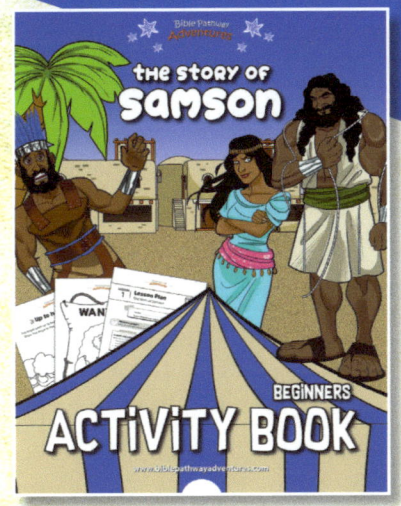
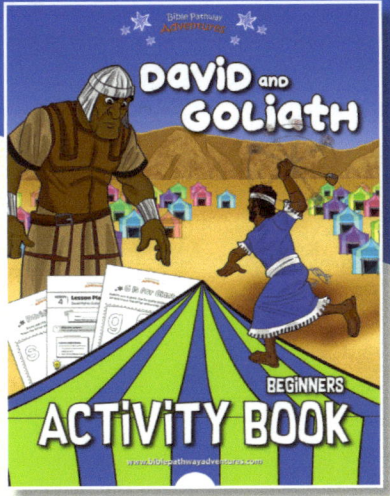
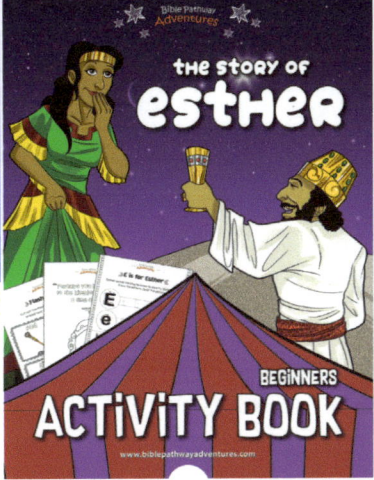
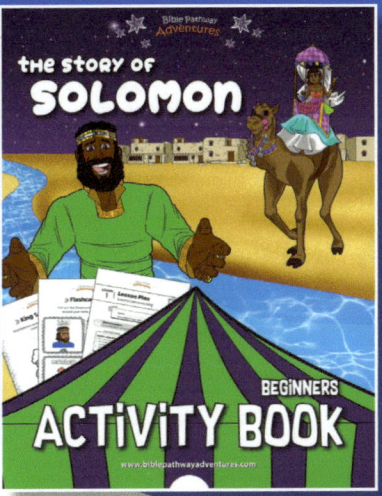
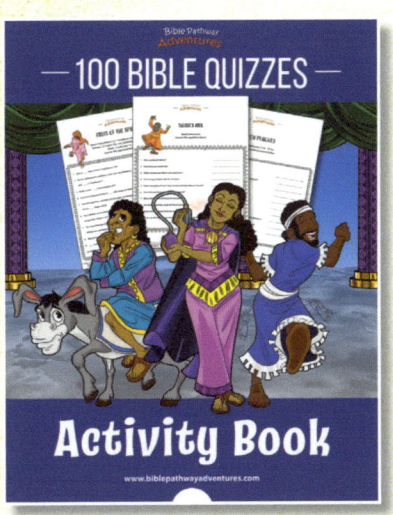

GO TO
www.biblepathwayadventures.com

www.ingramcontent.com/pod-product-compliance
Lightning Source LLC
Chambersburg PA
CBHW041324290426
44108CB00004B/121